Planet Dexter's

Calculator Mania!

101 Ways to Enjoy a Calculator

Without Throwing It!

Scholastic Inc.

New York   Toronto   London   Auckland   Sydney

Acknowledgments

Lisa, Sue, Lynda, Sandy, Carole, Tom, Amy,
Michael, Ben, Susanne, Tim, John, Brenda, Andy,
George, Margo, Tim, John, Kristen, and Al

ISBN 0-590-73165-3

12 11 10 9 8 7 6 5 4 3 2 1   6 7 8 9/9 0 1/0

Printed in the U.S.A.   08

First Scholastic printing, February 1996

Book design by Skolos/Wedell, Inc.
Nancy Skolos, Eric Baily, and E. Lokilani Lum-King

Illustration by Jack Keely

Here are the keys

you need to use in this book:

Five plus two equals seven.

5 + 2 = 7

Six point two divided by four equals...

6.2 ÷ 4 =

And the most important key of all:

OFF! to save your poor battery after you've been playing with your calculator all day.

C clears everything but the memory.

CE clears the last number you entered.

Note: To figure out what order you need to push the buttons talk through the problem in your mind like this:

To divide:
÷ means divide.

To multiply:
X means times.

To subtract:
— means minus.

To add:
+ means plus.

To get the answer:
= means equals.

• Puts a decimal point in a number.

And a Message – in non-lawyer words! – from the Editors of Planet Dexter:

- do not throw or eat the calculator

- do not fry up the book for dinner

- keep this book away from your pet porcupine.

The dictionary says that "mania" is an "intense enthusiasm."

That sounds about right because that's all Planet Dexter's Calculator Mania wants from you: to be enthusiastic about Calculator Mania. Beyond that there are no rules and regulations (just as there's no gravity on Planet Dexter). You can start on any page you wish.

You can sit, stand, lie down, snore, or jog when you enjoy this book (on Planet Dexter you can even jump twice as high). And you can use this book in any room, or outside, or in a doorway—half in and half out. As far as we're concerned, you don't even have to put Calculator Mania on the bookshelf when you're not using it—it's OK with us under your bed or mixed with your dirty laundry or even in the refrigerator.

But remember, the real purpose of Calculator Mania is that you enjoy a couple of minutes or hours of your life that you wouldn't have otherwise. So look, if you don't like Calculator Mania, let us know. Seriously. Really! *Please!* OK? Or better yet, let us know if you do like this book. Honestly! You can write to us at the following address:

The Editors of Planet Dexter
Addison-Wesley Publishing Company
One Jacob Way
Reading, MA 01867
Or, you can FAX us at (617) 944-8243 or even contact us via The Internet at pdexter@aw.com or America Online at PDexter.

Anyway, we do hope you enjoy *Calculator Mania* and that we'll soon hear from you. And remember, on Planet Dexter everybody's brain holds twice as much.

—The Editors of Planet Dexter

You can share this book or not share it. You can surely use it to get out of chores—that's why the calculator is there. Whenever you're using a calculator, you look as if you're doing something important, like homework, or calculating your million-dollar bank account, stuff like that. So parents will generally leave you alone if you're playing with this book. Being left alone can often be a very good thing.

Calculator Buttons Are Really Weird

Get a load of this:

1) Enter the numbers on the buttons across the bottom row of your calculator, from right to left, like this: **321**.

2) Then subtract the numbers in that row from left to right: **321-123**.

3) Did you get **198**?

1) OK, now do the same for the numbers in the middle row, again from right to left: **654**.

2) Now reverse the numbers in the middle row and subtract: **654-456**.

3) What did you get? **198**? Right!

1) Let's try the top row. Punch the buttons from right to left: **987**

2) Reverse and subtract: **987-789**.

3) BINGO! **198**!

So experiment. Go for it. Do whatever you want to try. What if you go up and down, entering **963-369** or **852-258**? What if you even go diagonally, punching **753-357**. What number keeps showing up when you subtract? Is it still **198**, or is it a new number? If it's a new number, can you divide it to produce **198**? **Wild!**

Same number. Bizarre, eh?

Pick out a number and see if you can then find consecutive numbers whose sum is that number. For example, pick the number **21**. Then think a bit... dum-dee-dum... and play with your calculator for a while... poke, poke, poke... and you might discover that

6 + 7 + 8 = 21 or that 10 + 11 = 21.

P L A Y Calculator

So now that you've got the right feel for this, pick any number. Or better yet, try the number **315**, which can actually be written as the sum of consecutive numbers in twelve different ways! Wow!

Here's a weird way to figure out how to do this: pick a number, say, **315** again. Then decide how many consecutive numbers you want to add together to get **315**. Let's say you want to try to add six consecutive numbers to get 315.

Divide 315 by 6 and get 52.5 on your calculator.

Now here's the tip: every time you divide your goal number **(315)** by an even number **(6)**, and get an answer that ends in 0.5, it's a sign that your proposed calculations will work. So just take the **52.5** and go down three numbers **(52, 51, 50)** and up three numbers **(53, 54, 55)** for a total of six numbers.

Now add them together: **50 + 51 + 52 + 53 + 54 + 55 = 315!!!!** Yay! Now dance around the room because it worked!

It's almost the same when you're trying to divide by an odd number of possible numbers, like **5** for instance. Say you want to see if there are five consecutive numbers that can add up to **315**. Divide **315** by **5** and get **63**. Because **63** is a whole number (it doesn't end in 0.5 the way 52.5 does), you find out that there are five consecutive numbers to add together to make **315**. Just count two down and two up from **63** to get five numbers, like so: **61 + 62 + 63 + 64 + 65 = 315!!!!**

YIPPEE! It really works!

Now try to do some on your own. *And hey, good luck!*

It's a Fact!! According to experts, "smart" kids watch the same TV shows that "average" kids do.

9

Calculating Dice

For this amazing feat, you need your calculator and three dice.

If you can't find three dice, annoy some grown-up until they give in and buy you *Planet Dexter's Shake, Rattle, and Roll: Games and Cool Things to Do with Dice that Grown-Ups Don't Even Know About.* This is yet another Planet Dexter book! It comes with free (well, sort of) dice. *Shake, Rattle, and Roll* is available at lots of bookstores.

And if you *still* can't find any dice, just write three numbers on a piece of paper—JUST BE SURE TO CHOOSE FROM THE FOLLOWING NUMBERS (the same as those on dice): 1, 2, 3, 4, 5, 6.

Now you, with the help of your calculator, will guess the three numbers that came up.

Really! You can do it!

It is against the law in Natchez, Mississippi, for elephants to drink beer.

OK, now get someone to roll the dice—but remember, don't look! (In the event that your pet porcupine ate all your dice for breakfast, just get someone to write down any three numbers that might show up if you had dice.)

Let's see . . . now where are we . . . oh, yes, that's right, the dice have just been rolled—remember, don't look at the dice! Give somebody the calculator and give these simple instructions. (Remember, don't look at the dice! It's the not looking that makes your performance here so impressive!)

Here are the instructions:

1) **Multiply the number on one of the dice by 2.**

2) **Add 5.**

3) **Multiply this result by 5.**

4) **Add a number from one of the other two dice.**

5) **Now multiply by 10.**

6) **Add the third number.**

7) **Get the calculator back.**

8) **You subtract 250.**

OK, you've just about done it. Start up a drum roll. You're almost there—on with the drum roll—faster!, louder! You have a three-digit number on the calculator. WHOA!— THEY ARE THE SAME THREE DIGITS THAT CAME UP ON THE DICE!! Cut the drums, hit the cymbals!!!!!!!

Phew!

How to Get Really **Rich**

with **Really** **Busy** **Parents**

in Only **30** **Days**

First, find a really busy parent.

Now be cool. Offer to do something **awful**, like cleaning the bathroom or washing the dishes or baby-sitting your kid brother (Really busy parents love this sort of stuff; they think you're "maturing." They phone neighbors and write to relatives, telling them all about how you must now have hormones—**GROSS!**) So if you don't act too excited, the average busy parent will jump at your offer without thinking.

Take a deep breath.

Again, remember, keep cool (it might be good to yawn about here, as if you're bored.) Now tell the really busy parent that you'll charge 1 cent (that's one penny AKA* 1¢ AKA "the old Lincoln head") the first day and that each day you'll charge twice as much as the day before. Even the not-so-busy parent might figure "let's see, that's one cent the first day, two cents the next day, and, uh, only four cents the next day, hey, sure, kid, sounds like a good idea.

*AKA="Also Known As"

Congratulations!

You've just done it. In thirty days, you'll be a multi-millionaire.

Really! Check it out on your calculator. Enter 0.01 (that's one cent for day one). Double that—multiply by 2—(that'll equal 0.02 and that takes care of day two). Double the 0.02 (that equals 0.04 on the third day). And keep going, doubling each day, for a total of 30 days. Look around throughout this book . . . *maybe* you'll find the specific work on this problem. Maybe.

So how much money are you owed on your thirtieth day?

Millions!!—right?

Awesome!!—right?

A really busy parent is a great thing to have around!!—right?

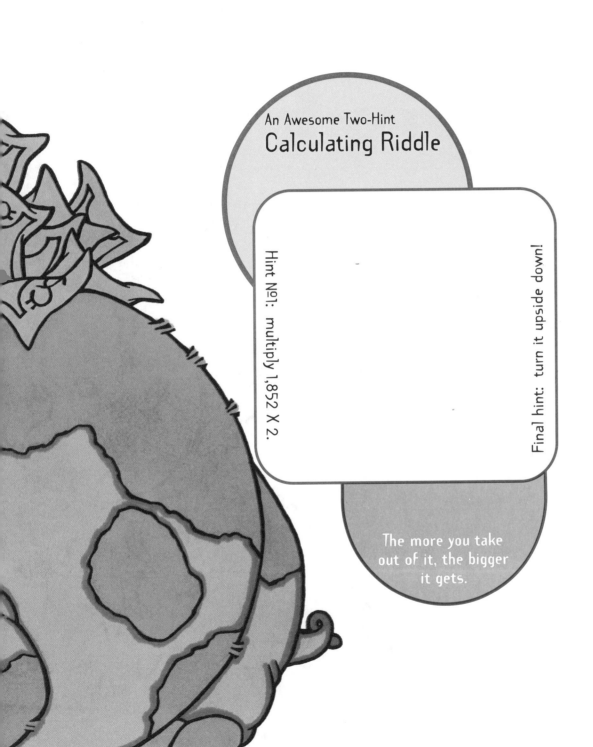

An Awesome Two-Hint
Calculating Riddle

Hint №1: multiply 1,852 X 2.

Final hint: turn it upside down!

The more you take out of it, the bigger it gets.

Riddles

Read this! There are riddles throughout this really strange book you now hold in your hands. It'll help an awful lot if you understand that when certain numbers are displayed by the calculator and then you turn the calculator upside down, those numbers look like specific letters of the alphabet. Really! No lie! For example, enter 4 Turn your calculator upside down. Says "h"—right? Or enter 3 and turn your calculator upside down. Says "E"—right? Or just to do one last example; enter 0 and turn yourself upside down (standing on your head is a popular method). Look at your calculator display.

[enter your name]'s . . .

Incredible
Magic Trick

(The title of this one is **all yours.** Really! Just stick in your name and confidently claim something like "I made up this trick last Tuesday night when I was bored for a few minutes" or maybe something else like "I discovered this quaint little trick while waiting for this morning's school bus. "So if you're Zoe, this is now known as "Zoe's Incredible Magic Trick," and if you're Burt, this is now known as "Burt's Incredible Magic Trick" . . . thata boy, Burt!)

Give someone your calculator and have this person punch in the number thirty-seven thousand thirty-seven. Then, just in case you mistakenly gave the calculator to some sort of alien idiot, you'd better check to see that the calculator actually reads **37,037**.

Now ask your number puncher for a favorite number between **1** and **9**. Whatever number you're given, multiply it by **3** in your head, and tell your number puncher to multiply **37,037**, which should already be in the calculator, by that number. So, for example, if your number puncher says **"4"** as a favorite number, you want to multiply by **12**. If you hear **"7,"** ask your number puncher to multiply by **21**. The answer will be a row of the favorite number. Really! Try it!

Then claim it as your own magic trick!

The Magic of 6,174

I'm like a kid. I'm special. There's no other number like me. Not at all. I'm **6,174**, and I'm the only number ever who can do the weird thing that follows. On your mark . . . get set . . . **GO!**

1) Pick four different numbers from 0 to 9.

   example ⟶ **4, 5, 6, 1**

2) Arrange them to make the largest number possible.

   6,541 ⟵ example

3) Now arrange them to make the smallest number possible.

   example ⟶ **1,456**

4) Subtract the small number from the large one.

   6,541
   −1,456
   ‾‾‾‾‾
   5,085 ⟵ example

5) Now, take the answer and arrange those numbers to make the largest number possible.   **8,550** ⟵ example

6) Now make the smallest number and subtract as you did above.

   example ⟶ **−0,558**
   ‾‾‾‾‾
   7,992

7) Continue to repeat these steps.
   example ——————

9,972
−2,799
‾‾‾‾‾
7,173

7,731
−1,377
‾‾‾‾‾
6,543

6,543
−3,456
‾‾‾‾‾
3,087

8,730
−0,378
‾‾‾‾‾
8,352

8,532
−2,358
‾‾‾‾‾
6,174

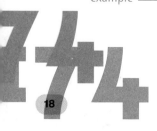

Tongue-
Twisting

Try this:

"The sixth sick sheikh's sixth sheep's sick."

THERE I AM! IF YOU KEEP DOING THIS, I ALWAYS

SHOW UP!

COOL, HUH!?

Day	Your Day's Earnings$$
1	0.01
2	0.02
3	0.04
4	0.08
5	0.16
6	0.32
7	0.64
8	1.28
9	2.56
10	5.12
11	10.24
12	20.48
13	40.96
14	81.92
15	163.84
16	327.68
17	655.36
18	1,310.72
19	2,621.44
20	5,242.88
21	20,485.76
22	20,971.52
23	41,943.04
24	83,886.08
25	167,772.16
26	335,544.32
27	671,088.64
28	1,342,177.20
29	2,684,354.40
30	5,368,708.80

grand TOTAL of what you've stiffed your really busy parents for: $10,737,417.67!!!

The following is offered by the Editors of Planet Dexter as a service to you, the reader, in the event that your really busy parents are suddenly demanding real "proof" now that they owe you (pause, take a deep breath, snicker to yourself) a grand total of **five million, three hundred and sixty-eight thousand, seven hundred eight dollars . . . and 80 cents.!!!!**

Hint №4: turn it upside down.

Hint №3: calculate 310 X 3 + 7.

Hint №2: jog.

Gym Class-
Calculating Riddle
Hint №1: take a walk.

Betcha You Can't Do This!

Arrange **eight 8**s so that the result is **1,000**:

888 + 88 + 8 + 8 + 8 = 1000

Arrange **seven 4**s so that the result is **100**:

44 + 44 + 4 + 4 + 4 = 100

Fill in the following question marks with either a plus sign or a multiplication sign:
9 ? 8 ? 7 ? 6 ? 5 ? 4 ? 3 ? 2 ? 1 = 100
(hint: aim for a pretty big number early in the calculation):

9 × 8 + 7 + 6 +5 + 4 + 3 + 2 + 1 = 100

Think for a Minute or Two

What if the distance between bases on a baseball field wasn't 90 feet. Just think about that. Ask yourself: "What if it had been 20 feet? Or 120 feet?" Would the game still be popular? More popular? Just think. Thinking is a good thing to do. For example, back to this baseball 90-feet thing: if the distance was instead 20 feet, wouldn't the field be smaller... which means that in an average stadium you could fit more seats...that means more people...more people eating stadium stuff like hot dogs...it only follows then that 20 feet between the bases would be better for the hot dog industry and in the end Oscar Meyer would be richer than Oscar already is. So you see, thinking is really a valuable thing to do.

A "How-to-Look-Really-Smart" Mini-Feature

This is a quickie, an in-the-hallways-between-classes sort of mind boggler. Pick any three-digit number from 100 to 999 and enter it twice into your calculator to produce a six-digit number. For example,

press 146; then **press 146** again. Your calculator **display will read 146,146**.

Now **divide by 7, divide** again **by 11,** and **divide** a third time **by 13**. Get a load of that!—the final answer is the same as your original three-digit number! This will always happen just as long as you're sure to pick a number between 100 and 999 and then divide that number by 7, then 11, then 13. Back to the example:

$$146{,}146 \div 7 = 20{,}878$$
$$20{,}878 \div 11 = 1898$$
$$1{,}898 \div 13 = 146.$$

Awesome

Those Strange Palindromes WOW!

Palindromes are numbers that read the same backward as forward—like 747. There are also palindrome words—like **WOW**. Now here's the interesting thing: with a calculator, you can create an infinite number of palindrome numbers. Really! Try this:

1) **Enter a three-digit number— for example, 236.**

2) **Reverse the number and add it to the first number: 236 + 632 = 868.** See the 868? That's your palindrome.

If you don't get a palindrome, keep trying. Keep reversing the answer and adding, so on and so on.

Let's try one of those:

$$
\begin{array}{r}
165 \\
+561 \\
\hline
726 \\
+627 \\
\hline
1,353 \\
+3,531 \\
\hline
4,884
\end{array}
$$

(This is your palindrome number.)

Those Strange Palindromes

wow!

Let's try some two-digit numbers:

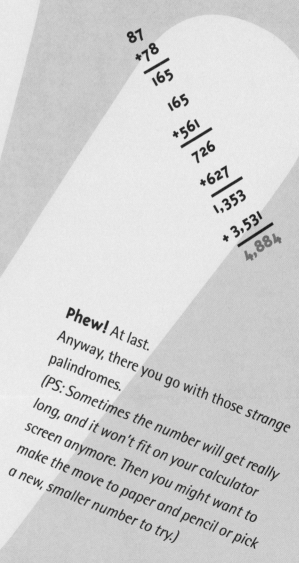

$$\begin{array}{r} 24 \\ +\,42 \\ \hline 66 \end{array}$$

$$\begin{array}{r} 87 \\ +\,78 \\ \hline 165 \end{array}$$

$$\begin{array}{r} 165 \\ +\,561 \\ \hline 726 \end{array}$$

$$\begin{array}{r} 726 \\ +\,627 \\ \hline 1{,}353 \end{array}$$

$$\begin{array}{r} 1{,}353 \\ +\,3{,}531 \\ \hline 4{,}884 \end{array}$$

Phew! At last. Anyway, there you go with those strange palindromes. (PS: Sometimes the number will get really long, and it won't fit on your calculator screen anymore. Then you might want to make the move to paper and pencil or pick a new, smaller number to try.)

Number

9

-- An Especially *Weird* Number Throughout History

For example, press $1 \div 9 =$,

then $2 \div 9 =$,

and then $3 \div 9$, and so on and so on . . . cool, eh?

Or better yet, pick any number that does not read the same backward and forward—so do not pick a number like 8,009,008 or 7,227 or 6.

Now write your number down so you don't forget it, and enter it on your calculator. Press the minus key and enter the same number again but backward. Now enter the equal key. Let's stop here and check an example in case you've somehow goofed this up already.

Example: $863,127 - 721,368 =$

Now back to yours. Write down the number showing on your calculator.

Example: $141,759$ ($863,127 - 721,368$) Good. Now clear your calculator screen. Then add up all the digits the answer contains. Let's again check in with our example:

press $1 + 4 + 1 + 7 + 5 + 9 = 27.$

now add the individual digits of that answer:

$2 + 7 = 9.$

Hey, how about that? It'll always be 9!

Here's a simpler example:
$54 - 45 = 9$

(PSST! Want to know something else that's cool about the number 9? All products of 9 have digits that can be added together to equal 9.

Like $9 \times 201 = 1,809$, so $1 + 8 + 0 + 9 = 27$, and $2 + 7 = 9$. Or $9 \times 6 = 54$, and $5 + 4 = 9.$

Cool.)

Another Turn-the-Old-
Calculator Riddle

Upside Down

Hint №1: It is hard to go up.

Hint №3: It is really just a big bump in the ground.

Hint №2: It is easy to come down.

77 x 100 + 9 + 5

Goof -a- Bit

1) Enter a number between 1 and 10 (remember what it is!!).

2) Multiply by 8.

3) Add 12.

4) Divide by 4.

5) Subtract 3.

6) Divide by 2.

7) Press the = button. Check the answer. Same number you started with—right? Pretty impressive—right?

25

A How-to-Psyche-Out-an-  Feature

Let's assume some **ATOP** is bugging you. Or perhaps somebody is *about* to bug you—maybe this afternoon you'll be stuck hanging out with some kid who is a lot better than you are at basketball (ugh!). The key here is to make **ATOP**s think they're unlucky, that no matter what they do today, they'll be haunted by bad luck.

First, tell the **ATOP** that you know a "scientifically proven mathematical formula" that determines somebody's luck. If at the completion of this formula, the calculator displays the very unlucky number 13, the **ATOP** can be sure to have bad luck for the next twenty-four hours. If at the end of the trick, however, any other number appears, everything will be OK.

*ATOP: **A**nnoying **T**ype **O**f **P**erson

Now what you know—and the **ATOP** doesn't know—is that you have a formula that always produces the very unlucky number 13. Really! Great, huh? So have your designated **ATOP** pick any three-digit number from 100 to 999. The **ATOP** should enter it twice into a calculator so that a six-digit number is displayed.

For example, if the **ATOP** picks 146, press
146 and then press 146 again. The calculator display will read 146,146.

Instruct the **ATOP** to divide that number
by 7. Then divide the answer by 11. Then
divide that answer by the original three-
digit number. Get a load of that!—the final
answer is 13! It always will be! Isn't
knowing that when **ATOP**s don't a
wonderfully sleazy thing?!?! Just remember: pick a number between 100 and 999;
then divide that number by 7, then 11,
then again by the original three-digit
number. Back to the example:

$$146,146 \div 7 = 20,878$$

$$20,878 \div 11 = 1,898$$

$$1,898 \div 146 = 13.$$

Awesome. Now your **ATOP** is in trouble.
All confidence is destroyed. Your **ATOP**'s
ego is out the window. Your **ATOP** will be
a nervous wreck and will most
likely forget about bugging you
for at least one day. And that surefire future
NCAA basketball star will probably volunteer
to skip this afternoon's game. So you see, the
calculator can be a pretty effective
thing to have around.

Just suppose there is an orchard of 172 apple trees, each averaging 332 branches, each with branch with 41 leaves at the beginning of May. New leaves are added to each branch at the rate of 10 per week. How many leaves will be on the tree after 8 months?

(answer see next page)

The Awesome

#7

Do the following problems on
your calculator and be sure
to write down each answer:

$1 \div 7 =$ _____

$2 \div 7 =$ _____

$3 \div 7 =$ _____

$4 \div 7 =$ _____

$5 \div 7 =$ _____

$6 \div 7 =$ _____

Get a load of that! In each answer, there
is a sequence of numbers that endlessly
repeats itself. See it? Right! It's
142,857. No other number does that.

142857142857142857142857
142857142857142857142857
142857142857142857142857

their leaves in the fall.
because trees shed
none
(answer)

This is a strange one.

Step #1: think—dum-dee-dum—of any three-digit number in which all digits are the same — for example, **333.**

Step #2: add the digits

(3 + 3 + 3 = 9)

Step #3: divide the number in step #1 by the number in step #2

(333 ÷ 9 = 37).

Hmmm, there's that 37. Let's try some others.

111 ÷ 3 = 37
222 ÷ 6 = 37
999 ÷ 27 = 37

Love it. Strange as all get out.

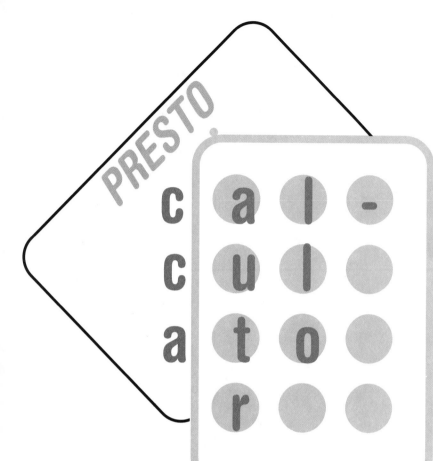

PRESTO

c a l c u l a t o r

Take whatever number is now on the calculator and subtract 5 from it. The **tens'** place of your final answer tells the number of the card (for the king, queen, and jack, the tens' and **HUNDREDS'** place will tell the number of the card). The ones' place tells the suit according to the numbers in step 5

Ask a friend to pick any card from a card deck. Everyone* except you should see the card. Your challenge is to use the calculator to guess that card. So give the person who picked the card the calculator and give these directions.

1) **Enter the card number (note:** <u>ace = 1</u>; <u>jack = 11</u>; <u>queen = 12</u>; <u>king = 13</u>).

2) **Multiply that number by 2.**

3) **Add 1.**

4) **Multiply by 5.**

5) **Add another number**

depending on which suit the card is: <u>clubs = 6</u>, <u>diamonds = 7</u>, <u>hearts = 8</u>, <u>spades = 9</u>.

6) **Ask to see the calculator with the answer showing.**

Let's do an example: suppose someone picks the 7 of clubs and 7 is entered. That's multiplied by 2 for 14. Adding 1 gives 15. Multiplying by 5 gets 75. Add 6 because it's a club, and that brings the number to 81. The calculator shows 81. You subtract 5 and get 76. The 7 is the number of the card; the 6 tells you that it's a club.

WHOA! Nifty!

* Let's think about that word "everyone": if you like to show off, do this in front of thousands at Yankee Stadium; if, on the other hand, you're a bit more selective about your audience, just do it with that original friend.

Calculating Riddle

№4

cost too much.

Hint №1: They come in pairs.

Hint №2: Grown-ups think they

Hint №3: 10609 x 5

So on Which Day of the Week Were You Born?

Even though you were surely there, you probably don't remember the day of the week on which you were born. Your parents may remember, but they've got a lot of really confusing things to be always thinking about, so you risk their memories failing on any one specific fact—especially one from years ago. So let's just figure it out ourselves by following six simple steps:

1) Write the last two digits of the year you were born. For example, let's pretend you were born on May 8, 1985. So you'd write the number 85.

2) Divide that number (85 in our example) by 4 and drop the remainder if there is one (85 ÷ 4 = 21.25, and drop the .25).

3) Find the number for the month in which you were born in the Table of Months (May = 2).

4) Find the day of the month on which you were born (8) (That was easy!).

5) Add the numbers from each of the first four steps (85 + 21 + 2 + 8 = 116)

6) Divide the answer from step 5 by the number 7 (116 ÷ 7 = 16.571428). What is the first digit of the remainder (just to the right of the decimal point) from this division? It's 5, and it should always be one of these numbers: 0, 1, 2, 4, 5, 7, 8. Find this remainder in the Table of Days.

Neat, eh? This will work for any birth date as long as it is in the twentieth century. You can't use it to find out days before 1900. So if you're talking to really old people, you might want to consider making a wild guess.

Table of Months

January	1	(0 in a leap year)
February	4	(3 in a leap year)
March	4	
April	0	
May	2	
June	5	
July	0	
August	3	
September	6	
October	1	
November	4	
December	6	

Table of Days

Sunday	1
Monday	2
Tuesday	4
Wednesday	5
Thursday	7
Friday	8
Saturday	0

C/O/D/E/ C/I/T/Y
Challenge

A = 1	J = 10	S = 19
B = 2	K = 11	T = 20
C = 3	L = 12	U = 21
D = 4	M = 13	V = 22
E = 5	N = 14	W = 23
F = 6	O = 15	X = 24
G = 7	P = 16	Y = 25
H = 8	Q = 17	Z = 26
I = 9	R = 18	

Using this code, you can write any word in numbers. Like CREEP would be 3 /18/ 5/ 5 /16 because **C = 3, R = 18, E = 5,** and **P = 16**. For purposes of the Code City Challenge, you'll need your calculator to multiply out a word. For example, to multiply out CREEP, you would enter 3 x 18 x 5 x 5 x 16. The answer is 21,600. So for purposes of the Code City Challenge, the value of CREEP is 21,600. The value of DOG is 420 (right?). And the value of UNDERWEAR is 219,088,800.

Now here's the challenge: find the word with the highest possible total— 99,999,999—*but without overloading your calculator!*

So CREEP's not so good, it totals only 21,600.
And UNDERWEAR's no good because it gives too big a number.
Try DRUDGERY. That gets you 5,292,000, which is OK.

34

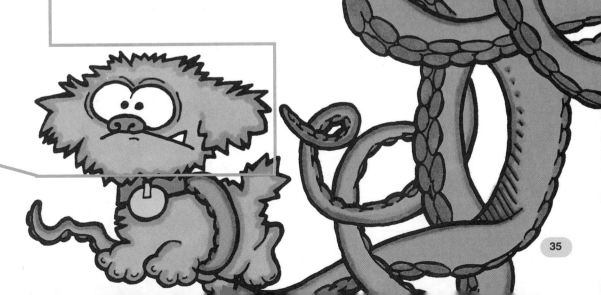

How about OCTOPUS? Wow—that's 90,288,000.

A major helpful hint: when you're looking for these "almost 99,999,999" words, keep a dictionary handy and look for words that are seven, eight, or nine letters long.

Top Ten (and one other) Dog Names

#1	Brandy
#2	Lady
#3	Max
#4	Rocky
#5	Sam
#6	Heidi
#7	Sheba
#8	Ginger
#9	Muffin
#10	Bear
#24,385	Planet Dexter

Drive Yourself:

CRAZY

Just suppose—use your imagination!—that suddenly, for more than a second or two, no one is bugging you. For once, no one is driving you **CRAZY!** Imagine that your parents and teachers are treating you like a member of the royal family. Imagine that little sisters, big brothers, and even strange cousins are showing you the respect you certainly deserve. And even imagine that *all* the school bullies are away on vacation—at the same time! Just imagine that. No one is driving you **CRAZY!**

But wait. Think about how it might feel. Hmmm . . . odd. A bit strange. Lonely. Even uncomfortable. If so, here's a way to bug yourself, to drive yourself **CRAZY!** It will let you get back to normal, to be once again your old irritable but fun-loving self!! Here goes. First enter a six-digit number in your calculator.

Now the trick is to get rid of that six-digit number in only four moves, using only two-digit numbers and only these four operations: x, +, -, ÷. (And hey, no multiplying or dividing by 0). Got that? Remember, each move consists of using a two-digit number and any one of the four basic math operations but none of that multiplying or dividing by 0 stuff.

Helpful hints: dividing early in the puzzle may decrease the number rapidly, but you risk developing decimal numbers which are difficult to eliminate. The best strategy is to get the number to a form that is evenly divisible and then divide.

Sample play (done by a 34-year-old electrical engineer!), using the six-digit number, **731,945:**

move 1:	÷ 99 =	7,393.3838
move 2:	÷ 20 =	369.66919
move 3:	÷ 13 =	28.436091
move 4:	- 28 =	0.436091

The electrical engineer **blew** it.

Now here's a sample play (developed and executed by a Planet Dexter editor!) using the six-digit number 180,000:

move 1:	÷ 90 =	2,000
move 2:	÷ 20 =	100
move 3:	- 10 =	90
move 4:	- 90 =	0 !!!

Five-Digits Weirdness

Take any 5-digit number—like 15658, or 22222, or Carrie Doyle's birth date which is 31772, or zip code (as long as it doesn't start with zero)—and multiply it by 11. Now multiply that answer by 9091. And holy smokers! Look at that answer!! It's that original 5-digit number—twice! For example:

$$15353 \times 11 = 584683 \times 9091 = 5315353153$$

WARNING: You may need a slightly fancier calculator (than your Planet Dexter model) for this weird thing to work perfectly.

Time Out
(from Calculators)

For this page, you don't need a calculator, which is great if your fingers are all sore and tired from pushing calculator buttons. "Time Out" is your basic two-person-guessing-but-full-of-strategy game. You'll need two players for this (you plus a friend or the neighborhood creep or a really smart dog will do). Each player thinks of a number—*a three-digit number is good for starters.*

For example, first you try and guess the really smart dog's number. Then after you've guessed the really smart dog's number (it can take quite a while, really!), switch roles. You get on the floor, and Rover (if that's the really smart dog's name, for example) hops onto the sofa. Then Rover tries to guess your three-digit number.

IMPORTANT NOTICE (hey! you! Listen up): Whenever one player makes a guess, the other gives some clues. Making good use of the clues is the place strategy comes in. There are three clues:

1) **GROSS** means that one of the guessed digits is correct but is in the wrong place.

2) **PERFUME** means that one of the guessed digits is correct and is also in the correct place.

3) **MONDO** means that none of the digits in the guess is correct.

If the guess contains more than one correct number, you give a combination clue, such as **GROSS PURFUME** or **GROSS GROSS.**

EVEN MORE IMPORTANT STUFF
(hey! you! Listen up):
1) If this gets too easy, move up to four-digit numbers . . . then five . . . and so on and so on.

2) Also think really seriously about dumping GROSS, PERFUME, and MONDO and instead creating your own clue words. Maybe use your real names, or better yet, make up words that can't be found in the dictionary, like "munchkernickle" or "bochagaloop."

Let's listen as a really smart dog and the neighborhood creep play a game, using the clue names suggested here.
The really smart dog is thinking of the number 224, and the creep is doing the guessing.

Creep	Dog (the number is 224)
"789"	
	"Mondo"
"456"	
	"Gross"
"432"	
	"Gross Gross"
"Aaa-chooo"	
	"Gesundheit"
"243"	
	"Gross Perfume"
"324"	
	"Perfume Perfume"
"124"	
	"Perfume Perfume"
"224"	
	"Got It!!!"

Animators drew nearly 6.5 million black dots for the film 101 Dalmatians.

39

Hand an EIP your calculator. Tell the EIP to enter the number **32,967.**

Now tell the EIP that you're going to flip-flop that number. The EIP will probably say **"wow!"**

Tell the EIP to multiply this number by its last digit, **7,** and divide by its first digit, **3.** The number will flip-flop. It'll become **76,923.** Cool, right? Really deserving of a "wow," and you're not even done. Keep going.

Tell the EIP now to multiply the new number (**76,923**) by its last digit (**3**) and divide that by the number's first digit (**7**). See that? You'll have flip-flopped back to **32,967.**

You can also do this trick with **1,089.** Really: 1,089 x 9 = 9,801 ÷ 1 = 9,801. And you can also do "The Old How to Impress EIPS" trick with the following numbers on the next page.

Your Aching Heart

2,178	21,978	219,978
3,267	32,967	329,967
4,356	43,956	439,956
6,534	65,934	659,934
7,623	76,923	769,923
8,712	87,912	879,923
9,801	98,901	989,901
10,989	109,989	

Now, all together: **"WOW!!!"**

*Here's a helpful suggestion for spotting EIPs (easily impressed people).

They say "wow" a lot and usually over nothing. Like the sun comes up in the morning, and they say, "Wow, kid, get a load of that sun!" Aunts and uncles who want you to like them are also easily impressed. They say stuff like "wow, dearie, you're so big;" and you know you're only two feet tall, the smallest kid in the whole school—yuck!

Your heart is, essentially, a pump. Its job is to push blood through about 60,000 miles of arteries, veins, and capillaries throughout your body. That's a lot of tubes! The muscles of your heart do a two-part squeeze (boom BOOM) together about eighty times a minute to give the blood a push. Each one of those double squeezes is called a heart-beat.

Using your calculator, can you figure out how many times a year your heart beats? Hint: it's a big number. More hints: remember that there are sixty minutes in an hour, twenty-four hours in a day, and 365 days in a year (366 if it's a leap year).

Really Easy Bonus!!! If your heart pumps 2,000 gallons per day, how much does it pump in a year? (Really BIG helpful hint: use your calculator!!!)

Here're some examples:

$$12 + 3 - 4 + 5 + 67 + 8 + 9 = 100$$

$$9 \times 8 + 7 + 6 + 5 + 4 + 3 + 2 + 1 = 100$$

$$2 \times 3 + 1 + 4 + 5 + 67 + 8 + 9 = 100$$

OK, now here's the **"Let's Make a Deal"** angle: if you come up with one of these use-all-nine-number-keys-to-get-to-100 things, send it along to the Editors of Planet Dexter (see "A Planet Dexter Sort of Introduction", EARLIER IN this book's "introduction" for our mailing address, our FAX number, and even our E-Mail address), and *maybe* we'll send you something in return. Cool, eh?

Let's Make a Deal

Obtain the number 100 on your calculator by

1) **Pressing each number key (1, 2, 3, 4, 5, 6, 7, 8, 9) only once**

2) **Pressing these other keys as often as you wish:** +, -, ÷, x, 0, =.

Let's pretend something gross and sticky got all over your calculator's number keys. Really gross. Really sticky. You can also pretend that this sticky, gross stuff also smells, really stinks—PHEW CITY!!! Anyway, this sticky, gross, smelly glop is all over your number keys—EXCEPT FOR THE 2 KEY and all the function keys, like - and + and ÷ and x and =. Yep, the glop missed the 2 key and the function keys. Now, here's the challenge:

Obtain 15 on your calculator's display by using no number keys other than the 2 . . . because, hey, there's just no way you're going to want to touch that glop stuff!!

Now, remember, you have to stick with the clean 2 key.

Give up? Here, try this: 22 ÷ 2 + 2 + 2. Neat, right?

THE TOP 10 CRAWLING GLOP SITUATIONS

Now, let's think of other situations —we'll call them **THE TOP TEN CRAWLING GLOP SITUATIONS—** in which only one number key is available (maybe all the other number keys are broken or the gross glop's crawled over to the 2 key, leaving the 1 key empty . . . ugh, just think about it . . . *crawling* glop!).

#10 Crawling Glop Situation

Get to 1 by pressing the same number key several times, other than 1, and not pressing any other number key.

#9 Crawling Glop Situation

Get to 2 by pressing the same number key three times, other than 2, and not pressing any other number key.

#8 Crawling Glop Situation

Get to 3 by pressing the same number key four times and not pressing any other number key.

#7 Crawling Glop Situation

Go for 4 by pressing 3 four times and not pressing any other number key.

#6 Crawling Glop Situation

End up with 30 by pressing 6 three times and not pressing any other number key.

#5 Crawling Glop Situation

Get to 37 in the display by pressing 3 five times and not pressing any other number key.

#4 Crawling Glop Situation

Obtain 100 in the display by pressing 9 six times and not pressing any other number key.

#3 Crawling Glop Situation

End up with 111 by pressing no number keys other than 2.

#2 Crawling Glop Situation

Go for 1,000 by pressing no number keys other than 8.

and the #1 Crawling Glop Situation

You have to go to the bathroom but there's not one around!

Answers to THE TOP TEN CRAWLING GLOP SITUATIONS

#1: pray

#2: $888 \div (888 - 8888)$ or $(8888 - 888) \div 8$

#3: $222 \div 2$

#4: $(99 \div 99) + 99$

#5: $(333 \div 3) \div 3$

#6: $(6 \times 6) - 6$

#7: $[(3 \times 3) + 3] \div 3$

#8: $(1 + 1 + 1) \div 1 \ldots$ and $(2 + 2 + 2) \div 2 \ldots$ and $(3 + 3 + 3) \div 3 \ldots$ etc. or $[(4 \times 4) - 4] \div 4$

#9: $(1 + 1) \div 1 \ldots (3 + 3) \div 3 \ldots (4 + 4) \div 4 \ldots$ etc.

#10: $2 \div 2 \ldots 22 \div 22 \ldots 3 \div 3 \ldots 33 \div 33 \ldots$ etc.

the calculating tale of you, a dead mosquito, and your little brother whom you unaffectionately call "the squirt"

Mosquitoes flap their wings 1,000 times every second. So grab your calculator, and let's have some fun with that. For example, assume that you're standing on Squirt, who is two feet tall; and Squirt's standing seven feet, six inches from the old window with the broken screen; and you're five feet tall, and your neck is ten inches from the top of your head; and there's no tailwind in the room; and a mosquito flies three feet per second. Therefore, how many times does a mosquito flap its wings between getting through the hole in the screen and landing on your neck?

Better yet, if the mosquito hadn't been so stupid to land on your neck, how many more times in its bloody life would it have flapped its wings between the time it landed on your neck and the exact moment at which you **SQUISHED** it!?

And last, once you suddenly **SCREAMED** then **SQUASHED** the mosquito with absolutely no warning to your little brother—remember, you're standing on him—for how many seconds or minutes thereafter did Squirt scream in terror?

Mosquitoes prefer biting you if you've just eaten a banana.

The Old How-to-Impress-a-Really-Stubborn-Twit Trick

Show the really stubborn twit a really stubborn number: 142,857. Really! This number hates to give up any of its figures. Seriously! Hand your calculator over to the stubborn twit. Have the twit multiply 142,857 by 2, or 3, or 4, or 5, or 6. See what happens? The number just rearranges its figures, never giving them up.

But be sure to stop short of multiplying the number by 7 because just as in seventh grade, strange things start to happen at this point.

The Free Calculator Ploy

Let's say you're in the mood for a new calculator—for whatever reason: maybe you can resell it for a tidy profit at the playground, or just like shoes, ears, and burgers, calculators are something you enjoy in pairs.

So here's a Planet Dexter sort of thing to do to get that additional calculator. Tell the wealthiest (greatly increases your odds) grown-up you can find, that your calculator is "stuck." Ask—with a sad, disappointed voice—for help "checking" the calculator, to make sure it is truly broken (sob, sob). Ask the grown-up to do these steps:

1) Enter the number 142,857.

2) Multiply it by 3 and hit the equals sign.

3) Subtract 1 from that and hit the equals sign.

4) Divide that by 10 and hit the equals sign.

5) Add 100,000 to that and hit the equals sign.

1) Again, enter the number 142,857.

2) Multiply it by 2 and hit the equals sign.

3) Subtract 14 and hit the equals sign.

4) Divide by 100 and hit the equals sign.

5) Add 30,000 and hit the equals sign.

6) Add 110,000.

Voila!! Up comes the same number the wealthy grown-up started with: 142,857. Hmmm, seems to be stuck. Now, act innocent here, as if this is all a mystery to you, that your poor, dear, old calculator is really broken . . . you might want to say, with a sigh, "well, let's try something else and see how that goes." Ask the wealthy grown-up to do these steps:

Wow! It's 142,857 again! *(Hey, it's beginning to look really stuck, right?)* Say something like "let's try another one, just to be sure." Ask the wealthy grown-up to do the following—*and make sure your grown-up enters the equals sign after every move:*

1) Enter the number 142,857.
2) Multiply by 6.
3) Subtract 142.
4) Divide by 1,000.
5) Add 30,000.
6) Add 112,000.

Holy smokes!—it's 142,857 again. In the event that you're dealing with that most frustrating of sorts—the wealthy *and* *stubborn* grown-up—try yet another (remember: make sure she enters the "equals" sign after every move): Have the wealthy *and* *stubborn* grown-up:

1) Enter 142,857.
2) Multiply by 4.
3) Subtract 1428.
4) Divide by 10,000.
5) Add 30,600.
6) Add 112,200.

Boom! There it is again, the old 142,857. Wow! This dude is stuck for sure.

Now remember, if at this point, that wealthy grown-up does not rush out and buy you another calculator, well, hey, it probably was never meant to be.

Thobe Sobecrobecoby Fobactobor
(or, The Secrecy Factor)

WIDDAGATCH IDDAGOUT!

3 For example, this message was recently distributed across the planet

2 Such times demand your own secret language. That's cool. It's done all the time on Planet Dexter.

1 Sometimes something's no one's business but yours and a friend's or a couple of friends.

50

Widdagatch iddagout! Thiddagat twiddagit, thiddage ciddagorpiddagoriddagate ciddagensiddagor, iddagis viddagisiddagitiddaging hiddageadquiddaguartiddagers tiddagodiddagay.

(If you figure this message out, great! And hey, let us know—see "A Planet Dexter Sort of Introduction" back earlier in this book, for our mailing address, our FAX number, and even our E-mail address. And *maybe* we'll send you something in return. Maybe.)

Here's a FREE (!) simple secret language suggestion you can use!

Stick  in front of the first vowel in each syllable.

Really. It's cool. It's what was done in the previous title; that's how "The Secrecy Factor" became "Thobe Sobecrobecoby Fobactobor." See? Hey, say it. Try it again. And again, real fast!!!! That's neat, too, right? It sounds goofy but works! Hey, just like life! Here's another FREE (!) suggestion. Practicing your secret language in the middle of otherwise normal or excellent behavior is the sort of thing that can drive other people nuts. Great, eh? Think about it. There you are, being a good, bright, better-than-average calculator whiz, yet that annoying **ob!** sound is scattered all through your sentences.

For example, gather yourself, at least one innocent victim, your calculator, and some of your friends who share a secret language (in this case, the **ob** language), and proceed with the following (after we give your friends the names: Zoe, Lola, Jack, and Annie):

You, to the grown-up:

"Enter a two-digit number."

You, to Zoe:

"**Obentober thobat obinnobocobent vobictobim's boborobing nobumbober twobo mobore tobimes sobo thobat yobou've gobot oba sobix-dobigobit nobumbober oband pobass thobe cobalcobulobatobor tobo Loboloba.**"

You, to Lola:

"**Dobivobide thobat nobumbober boby throbee oband pobass thobe cobalcobu- lobatobor tobo Joback.**"

You, to Jack:

"**Dobivobide thobe nobumbober obon thobe cobalcobulobatobor boby sobevoben oband pobass thobe cobalcobulobatobor tobo obAnnobie.**"

You, to Annie:

"Dobivobide boby thobirtobeen oband pobass thobe cobalcobulobatobor boback tobo thobe obin-nobocobent vobictobims."

You, to the grown-up:

"Divide by 37 and read the number in the display."

Get a load of this—it'll be the two-digit number that the goofy grown-up originally entered in the calculator! Great!

Essentially, this entire process, includ-

ing the calculator wizardness and all the "**ob**-ing," will stun the innocent victim into a noncommunicative state for days. Thus, this is a helpful activity to employ just prior to a situation that simply requires the removal of somebody—maybe some understanding grown-up—from the course of events for a period of several days. Then feel free to welcome the person back. People like that.

Another Awesome Calculator Riddle

Hint Nº1: They're like the Empire State Building

Hint Nº2: And like Shark teeth, Patrick Ewing, and my neighbor's ears:

51 x 18

Here's an example of the math for this procedure (assume the goofy grown-up's two-digit number is 75):

757,575 ÷ 3 ÷ 13 ÷ 7 ÷ 37 = 75.

GROSS BUT GREAT!!!! To create the language of the mutants in the 1932 film, Island of Lost Souls, a mixture of animal sounds and foreign languages were recorded then played back at alternating speeds. The sound caused audiences to vomit in the theaters.

You know

those cards that are always falling out of magazines, those cards asking you to subscribe to the magazine for twelve months or whatever. *People in the magazine industry* call them "blow-in cards." *Normal people*—like people who read this book—call them **"annoying,"** because they're always falling out, messing up your backpack, or trashing the car's backseat or your locker.

Hey, think about this: maybe you could get fined or arrested for littering because of those annoying blow-in cards. For example, you could be walking home from the newsstand with some magazines and just as you walk past the police station, those blow-in cards start falling out. Maybe ten of them. Police rush out of the station and start fining you **$100** for each piece of litter. That could be a lot of money. Figure it out on your calculator. Wow! That's $1,000*, right? That hardly seems fair.

*10 x $100 = $1,000

So do not do this: put every blow-in card you can find into a mail box, because, you see, the magazine—not you—pays for the mailing, so that's going to cost those fancy magazines lots of money. Really. Get your calculator. Let's assume everybody who reads this book ignores the advice NOT to do this and actually DOES DO IT. And let's assume 50,000 kids read this book and each kid puts thirty blow-in cards into the mail, and the postage on each card is 19 cents. Work it out on your calculator. Wow! That's going to cost a lot! $285,000, right?**

Of course if people were to do this—*not that we're suggesting anybody do it*—they wouldn't have to fill in any of the card's blanks, like name or address, because the post office mails them back to the magazines, at their cost, whether the cards are blank or not.

Anyway, remember that the advice presented here, not to do what we've just explained how to do, is simply another free service from the Editors of Planet Dexter.   You're welcome.

**50,000 x 30 x 19 cents

Bats always turn left when exiting a cave.

The Truly Excellent Crossword Puzzle

Did you know that your calculator can make words? **Really!** Just type in certain numbers, turn your calculator upside down, and wow, those numbers look like letters of the alphabet! **For example, enter 4.** Turn your calculator upside down. **Says "h" right? Or enter 3** and turn your calculator upside down. **Says "E"—right?**

This trick can be really useful in school when you want to pass a note to a friend. Here's what you do: just type in some numbers (an upside-down word), and hand it over, and if you get caught, you and your pal look like serious scholars sharing an equation.

There aren't that many letters that you can make with your calculator, so you have to choose your words carefully and use some imagination when you're reading them. Ignore the decimal points, for instance, and consider that some of the upside-down numbers make capital letters and some make lowercase letters. Just cut the poor calculator some slack, and it will serve you well as a secret communication tool. Anyway... enough of our blabbing...

CHECK OUT THIS CROSSWORD PUZZLE!

ACROSS

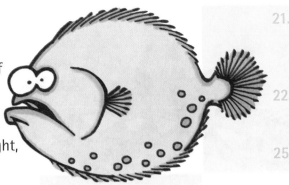

1. If a friend stares at your candy bar as if he really wants it, he _____ it.
   (2 x 26,500) + 90 + 700

4. Short for Island, like, the _____ of Wight, the _____ of Man.
   (750 x 5) + 1

7. Strange, old-time comic-strip character: _____' Abner.
   (111 x 7) – 60

8. What you're supposed to say when you pick up the phone: "_____?"
   (7,000 + 17 + 17 + 700) ÷ 10,000

10. A verb, My brother _____ loud. My room _____ cool. My dinner _____ gross.
    (25 x 2) + 1

15. The Bulls have had three wins and only one _____.
    2500 + 2500 + 250 + 250 + 7

16. Punky Brewster's real name; it means "sun" in French.
    (350,000 x 2) + 13705

18. My brother is such a pig. He _____ the whole couch when we play SEGA.
    (2,500 x 2) + 452 + 452

19. I thought my mom was going to keel over when she saw the phone _____.
    (35 – 17) + 350 + 350 + 3500 + 3500

20. You couldn't stop laughing. You had a serious case of the _____.
    900 + 18 + 1 + 379,000 + 5,000,000

21. When you have a lemonade stand, you _____ lemonade.
    (7 x 5) + 350 + 7,350

22. Where some animals are kept behind bars.   2 ÷ 100

25. A 200-pound candy bar. A 12-gallon ice cream sundae. A 1,200-page book. Arnold.
    51 x 18

27. Sticky stuff.
    9 ÷ 100

28. OK, here's a freebie: same as 59 Down.

29. What a fish breathes through.
    3,500 + 3,500 + 350 + 350 + 3 + 5 + 3 + 5 + 3

31. A garden tool.
    (101 x 3) + 1

32. What you use to start a fire in a fireplace.
    (3 x 300) + 3 + 3 + 1

33. If you like things to be messy, other people might call you a _____
    323 x 25

36. Tall, round building where corn is kept. Also the name of a storage place for nuclear bombs.
    (143 x 5) ÷ 1000

37. A kind of car. A nickname for the study of maps.
    (3 x 13) ÷ 100

38. You're kind of tired, kind of bored. You let out a long breath called a _____.
(2500 x 2) – 85

42. The Beauty's name in *Beauty and The Beast*. A geeky old-fashioned expression calls a popular girl the _____ of the ball.
26,627 + 11,111

52. The opposite of she.
11 + 11 + 11 + 1

53. If you're not blind, you can _____.
67 x 5

54. Your brother pleads to stay up as late as you. He even gets down on his knees and _____.
(3,000 x 2) – 62

55. Does this sound familiar? "Clean up your room or _____!"
(715 x 5) – 2

57. Hens lay 'em.
(1,000 – 7) + 5,000

60. The Houston _____ers. _____ of Olay. Wesson _____.
142 x 5

61. In the book and movie *Charlie and the Chocolate Factory*, Willy Wonka has a _____ that lays a golden _____.
(99,300,000 + 35,000 + 9) ÷ 100,000

44. Candy suckers on sticks, without the pop.
(1,063,540 x 5) + 7

47. These make noise on a snow vehicle (a two-part clue).
1) 380,264 + 111,111
2) 28,869 x 2

DOWN

2. The lion represents this astrological sign.
(40 – 3) ÷ 100

3. What you plant stuff in to make it grow.
(700 x 5 x 2) + 105

5. A kind of fish or the bottom of your high-top.

$(2{,}000 \times 2) - 295$

6. What you say when you want a pest to leave you alone.

$(3 \times 3 \times 5) \div 1{,}000$

7. The star of *Naked Gun*'s real first name (hint: this is a name for boys and girls).

$(600{,}000 \div 2) + 17{,}000 + 537$

9. _____and behold!

$(3 + 3 + 1) \div 10$

11. Vegetables are _____good (NOT!).

$(2 + 2 + 1) \div 10$

12. You can climb up it and sled down it.

$(77 \times 100) + 7 + 7$

13. Santa's belly laugh.

$(20{,}202 \times 2) \div 100{,}000$

14. This is what you do to make a liquid hot, but it also means "big, pus-filled sore".

$3{,}500 + 3{,}500 + 50 + 50 + 4 + 4$

17. You can usually find a knee in the middle of one.

$(310 \times 3) + 7$

18. The opposite of "hers."

$250 + 250 + 14$

19. When this rings, class is finally over.

$6{,}627 + 1{,}111$

23. What you dig when you want to bury something.

$1{,}500 + 1{,}500 + 350 + 350 + 2 + 2$

24. Fact: they found a totally preserved ancient dead guy in one of these in Scotland.

$(30 \times 30) + 4 + 4$

25. This is what digests your food. Some of it comes out when you throw-up.

$22{,}308 \div 6$

26. Part of a window that you can keep stuff on.

$1{,}543 \times 5$

27. Baby Talk.

$9009 \div 100{,}000$

28. Your sister can't tell you what to do. She's not the _____.

$(11{,}000 \div 2) + 2 + 2 + 2 + 2$

30. If you can't find these, you'll have to go barefoot.

$10{,}609 \times 5$

34. Sometimes, you can be so funny that it truly _____the mind.

$(101 \times 3) + 379{,}605 + 5{,}000{,}000$

35. This is what they call the bathroom in England. In number form, it's James Bond's code number.

$(10 - 3) \div 100$

36. You can find them on the beach. A little clam condo or a mussel mansion.
$(154{,}000 \div 2) + 9 + 9 + 9 + 9 + 9 + 300$

39. A round ice house that some people live in on the North Pole.
$791 \div 10{,}000$

40. A really cool woodwind instrument that you hear in an orchestra or a band.
$(4 \times 800) - 120$

41. This sticky gunk keeps your hair in place and can give you the "wet look".
$350 + 350 + 35 + 4$

43. They sting, but they also make honey.
$1{,}185{,}036 \div 222$

45. _____ no! I lost my homework again!
8×5

46. The guy who plays the Six Million Dollar Man in those old reruns has a first name that guys or girls can have. His name is _____ Majors.
$(111 \times 3) + 4$

48. Oh my _____! Osh Kosh B' _____!
$(9{,}000 \div 2) + 3 + 3 + 3$

49. This is the last giveaway: same barfy stuff you found in 25 down.

50. Telling them gets you into lots of trouble.
$(2660 \times 2) - 3$

51. One of those flower chains that you get to wear in Hawaii.
$1{,}000{,}000 - 999{,}863$

52. A quick hello.
$(3 \times 7) - 7$

56. These are totally gross and slimy, and some are even deadly, so beware. (P.S. Lots of people eat these. Yuck!)
$(3 \times 11) + 700 + 5{,}000$

58. An old-time expression: _____ whiz!
$(113 \times 9) \div 3$

59. Ghosts say this.
$8 \div 100$

The Best Ever Don't-Need-a-Calculator-or-Dice-or-Cards-or-Teacher Trick—
Perfect for Freds

- Ask a friend (let's pretend his name is Fred) to think of a number between 1 and 10 (but make sure that Fred doesn't tell you the number!!).

- Tell Fred to multiply that number by 9 (but again, Fred keeps his mouth shut, doesn't tell a thing).

- Fred should then add the two digits of the product together (for example, if Fred originally picked 8 and he multiplied that by 9, he's now at the number 72. Add the 7 and 2 together to get 9).

- At this point in the "Best Ever Don't-Need-a-Calculator-or-Dice-or-Cards-or-Teacher Trick," anybody will be at the number **9.** They have to be. Even if it's Fred, Ben, Helen, or Boopsie. Because when you multiply any number between 1 and 10 by 9, the digits of the answer always totals **9**. Really. Think about it. **9, 18, 27, 36, 45, 54, 63, 72, 81, 90.** Great, right? Because now you've got Fred right where you want him. You're controlling this trick. You're running the show. And he doesn't know what's going on! **Not at all!**

● Let's continue. Tell Fred to subtract 5 from the number he now has. But again, he's not to tell you the answer. Which, **of course, you know is 4.** Right? (Because you always have 9 at this point and 5 subtracted from 9 is always 4.)

● Ask Fred to assign a letter to the number they end up with: a = 1, b = 2, c = 3, d = 4.

At this point, Fred will always be thinking of "d". Right? But not telling you, right?

● Ask Fred to think of a country in Europe that starts with that letter (Fred will be thinking of Denmark because that's the only country in Europe that starts with a "d"). But he's still keeping his mouth shut, right?

● Now ask Fred to think of an animal that starts with the second letter of the country he is thinking of. We know Fred's thinking of Denmark (after all, we got him to this point without him even knowing it), so we know he's trying to come up with an animal that starts with the letter "e". Most everybody will think of "elephant."

● We're almost there. Ask Fred to think of the color of that animal (note: all elephants are "gray").

● Now you're set to stun Fred. Here goes. (drum roll) Ask him if he's thinking of a "gray elephant from Denmark".

This almost always works. Unless Fred can't add, subtract, or multiply; or if he doesn't know the countries of Europe; or if he's some weirdo who thinks of "eel" instead of "elephant"; or if Fred thinks elephants are green.